Colin Pomeroy was born in Dorset, and now lives at Tincleton, near Dorchester. He is a Vice-President of the Society of Dorset Men, following his return to the county after a career as a pilot in the Royal Air Force and, later, in civil aviation. His historical interests extend beyond the scope of this book to military and transport history, and he is the author of *Military Dorset Today* (1995).

Following page
The south-west gatehouse at Sherborne Old Castle, seen from within the bailey and before English Heritage had carried out major restoration work.

DISCOVER DORSET

CASTLES AND FORTS

COLIN POMEROY

THE DOVECOTE PRESS

The ruins of Rufus Castle, Portland, in 1786.

First published in 1998 by The Dovecote Press Ltd
Stanbridge, Wimborne, Dorset BH21 4JD

ISBN 1 874336 59 9

© Colin Pomeroy 1998

Colin Pomeroy has asserted his rights under the Copyright, Designs
and Patent Act 1988 to be identified as author of this work

Series designed by Humphrey Stone

Typeset in Sabon by The Typesetting Bureau
Wimborne, Dorset
Printed and bound by Baskerville Press, Salisbury, Wiltshire

3 5 7 9 8 6 4 2

CONTENTS

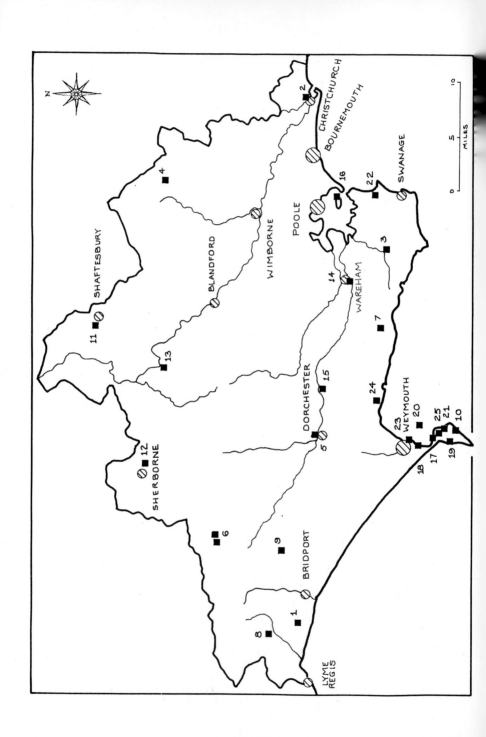

INTRODUCTION

Dorset's strong military connections are emphasised by the county's badge: a castle above an heraldic shield and the motto 'Who's Afear'd'. This book includes all twenty-five of the county's castles and forts that remain in some form or other today and which can claim, to a greater or lesser extent, to have been built or adapted for military purposes. The castles and forts of the post-Roman, Tudor and Victorian periods are described separately, for in each of these phases in the county's history the structures differ in both building design and associated defensive concept. Their range is wide, stretching west to the Marshwood Vale, east to Christchurch, north to Sherborne and as far south as the Isle of Portland.

Each castle or fort is unique, and has its own story to tell – be it of combat and intrigue, seige and foray, or valour and bravery – and time has been kinder to some than to others. Equally, history has left us more detailed accounts of some of the castles and forts than of others, and this is reflected in the varying lengths of each entry in the book.

It is appropriate to mention what is not included in this guide. Interesting as they might be in their own right, it does not cover buildings calling themselves castles, but which are castles in name

Opposite page Key to Dorset's Castles and Forts:
1. Chideock Castle, 2. Christchurch Castle, 3. Corfe Castle, 4. Cranborne (Castle Hill) Castle, 5. Dorchester Castle, 6. East Chelborough Castles.
7. Lulworth Castle, 8. Marshwood Castle, 9. Powerstock Castle, 10. Rufus (Bow and Arrow) Castle, 11. Shaftesbury Castle, 12. Sherborne (Old) Castle, 13. Sturminster Newton Castle, 14. Wareham Castle, 15. Woodsford Castle, 16. Brownsea (Branksea) Castle, 17. Portland Castle, 18. Sandsfoot Castle, 19. Blacknor (West Wears) Fort, 20. Chequer (Breakwater) Fort, 21. East Wears Battery, 22. Fort Henry, 23. Nothe Fort, 24. Upton Fort, 25. Verne Citadel.

The oriel window and porch, Highcliffe Castle. Highcliffe is a perfect example of a 'mock' castle built without any military purpose: others in Dorset include Pennsylvania Castle on Portland (built 1790s), Wyke Castle (early nineteenth century) and Durlston Castle near Swanage (1880s). Highcliffe Castle was built in the 1830s by Lord Stuart de Rothesay. It was destroyed by a succession of fires in the 1960s and is now undergoing restoration by Christchurch Borough Council with help from public funds.

only (Wyke and Highcliffe Castles, for example). Nor does it include the royal hunting manor at Gillingham, which, despite claims to the contrary, had no defensive purpose and cannot be labelled a castle. Equally, it excludes sites where it is definitely known that a castle existed, but of which there is no trace today (such as Bridport

Castle). Nor, of course, does this book attempt to cover Dorset's Iron Age hillforts (such as Maiden Castle), as they have no connection with what is traditionally considered to be either a castle or a fort.

Regardless of the era in which they were built, castles and forts owe much in their design to the effectiveness of the weaponry with which the resident garrison tried to defend itself, and to the weapons with which they were attacked. Longbows, crossbows, muskets, and cannon, as they were developed, became available to both sides. Boiling oil, tar and pitch poured from overhanging galleries added to' the defensive armoury, whilst seige cannon, assault towers, battering rams and mining were, at various times, in the inventory of the assailants. But of all the developments which had a major effect on fortress design, two stand out as the most important: the invention and refinement of gunpowder (between the early years of the four-teenth century and the mid-seventeenth century) and the introduc-tion of breech-loading, rifled-barrel artillery. The former meant that defensive structures were vulnerable in ways unthought of in earlier times, whilst the latter improved rates of fire, accuracy and effective engagement ranges to such an extent that warfare was revolutionised. In the early days of the castles we are considering the besieging forces would normally have only achieved victory over a defending garrison by starving it out, by cutting off its water supply, or by treachery.

Today the forts and castles of Dorset remind us of times of both local strife and international conflict; none of them, though, still serves any military function. Nevertheless, the county still has a part to play in the defence of the realm. The Royal Marines have a base at Poole; the Army has major bases at Blandford, Bovington, East Lul-worth and West Moors; and Territorial Army units – today's equiv-alent of the militia of yesteryear – are spread throughout the county. None occupies a fort in the traditional sense, for modern warfare has made such defensive structures obsolete, but the barbed wire coils. surveillance cameras and armed guards serve to remind us that the soldiers of the twenty-first century still need a secure perimeter from behind which to operate.

THE SAXON AND MEDIEVAL
CASTLES

The earliest post-Roman fortified strongholds in Dorset that can be precisely identified are the defences laid out by King Alfred following his victory over the Vikings at the Battle of Edington, Somerset, in 878. Of the three in Dorset, those at Shaftesbury and Christchurch evolved into true castles in the wake of the Norman Conquest, whilst the earth ramparts he ordered to be built at Wareham still enclose much of the modern town, particularly to the north and south.

The earliest castles constructed in the wake of the Norman invasion were primarily built for defence. They also acted as a visible symbol of the authority of the local landowner, with much of this authority coming directly from the good offices of the Crown. Known as 'motte-and-bailey' castles, they were, with rare exceptions, built on high ground and consisted of an inner keep – usually atop a motte – and an outer defensive wall, or bailey. The earliest used local timber in their construction, which was gradually replaced by stone as both a means of strengthening the structure and of resisting attack by fire. When the lay of the land permitted it, the castle would have been surrounded by a moat or dry ditch.

These castles survived for a varying number of years: some only a decade or two; others as late as the Civil War. The present state of their remains is equally variable. Some are barely discernible residual earthworks, others are impressive ruins of international importance.

Location: Alongside the public footpath running north from the village of Chideock, on the A35, towards North Chideock.
OS Reference: SY 424931.
Viewing: Unrestricted. The easiest access is via Ruins Lane, Chideock; alternative access is from North Chideock (where car parking is more readily available).

Following a raid by French shipping in 1377 on the coastal port of Weymouth, Sir John Craddock obtained permission to turn his manor house on the north side of Chideock village into a fortified castle. It was enclosed by a square moat, with outer defences to the

The engraving by Nathaniel and Samuel Buck of Chideock Castle in the 1730s before the final destruction of the gatehouse.

south and west, and possibly a tower at each corner. There are no records to show whether the castle was ever called upon to thwart the advances of marauding mariners, but it certainly saw action during the Civil War, over 250 years later. Held initially by supporters of Charles I, it fell to the Roundheads in March 1643, returned to Royalist control in December 1644 and finally succumbed to Parliamentary forces in July 1645, when 100 prisoners and their arms, including three barrels of powder, were also taken. Following this final battle, Parliament ordered the castle to be destroyed, a task undertaken by the Governor of Lyme Regis, Colonel Ceely, for the sum of £1/19s (£1.95p).

Although this eliminated Chideock Castle's usefulness as an armed stronghold, the destruction was not complete, for it was not until 1741 that the gatehouse was finally razed. An engraving of 1733 by Nathaniel and Samuel Buck dramatically portrayed the ruins as they were before their final demise.

With time all the stone has been removed from the site for building purposes elsewhere, and today no single piece of the original masonry remains. However, the undulating banks, mounds and ditches are obviously of military origin, and this historic site is commemorated by a wooden cross mounted on a stone plinth erected by Colonel Humphrey Weld in the mid-1950s, and later replaced with the present cross by his son, Charles, in 1993. Today the meadow where Chideock Castle once stood is but a haven of pastoral bliss on the edge of a traffic-plagued village.

CHRISTCHURCH CASTLE

Location: Alongside the minor road between Christchurch town centre and the suburb of Purewell.
OS Reference: SZ 163926.
Viewing: Fully accessible from local pathways.

In the ninth century King Alfred erected an earthwork on the banks of the River Avon, where the Saxon Square car park now stands, as a defence against marauding Danish sea raiders, but building and development over the years leave us with no traces of it today.

The ruins of Christchurch Castle's stone keep stand on top of an earth motte. Together with the Constable's House, Christchurch Priory, and the nearby River Avon, the castle ruins form one of the most attractive urban landscapes in Dorset.

The current castle ruins at Christchurch, or Twynham (or Twineham) as the settlement was first known, date back to Norman times. It was originally built of timber on top of an earth motte, and stood behind behind an outer defensive wall which extended down to the River Avon. The stone keep, the remains of the 10 feet (3 m) thick walls which we see today, are of late twelfth century origin. When completed the castle was fully enclosed by a moat and curtain walls, and was unique in Dorset in having a secondary moat between the motte and the outer courtyard. It is interesting to note that much of the stone was brought to Christchurch from the Isle of Wight and not quarried on the mainland.

The twelfth century Constable's House at Christchurch Castle, with the base of the garderobe tower prominent in the foreground.

Nearer to the river, on the banks of the mill stream, stand the remains of a building erected, probably around 1162, by Richard de Rivers, Earl of Devon, and used as the Constable's House and as a hall for the castle. It was entered on the first flooor via an external staircase (now gone). The garderobe tower, in the south-east corner over the mill stream, was a thirteenth century addition.

Before the castle was fully completed it was fought for during the twelfth century conflict between King Stephen and Empress Maud, and it has seen its fair share of combat over the years. In 1307 specific instructions were issued to 'keep secure and defend the castle when the King leaves our shores for foreign parts'. During the Civil War it was held initially for the Royalists by Sir John Mills, but fell to Roundhead forces without a fight in 1644 (when some 400 prisoners were taken) and two further attempts later in the year to regain it for Charles I met with no greater success.

It was decided in May 1650 to demolish the castle, a task the Governor of Southampton was instructed to carry out. It was, however, only following complaints that the castle's guns were still there and unguarded, that in July 1651 he actually removed the weaponry and completed the demolition! The hall, in contrast, has merely succumbed to the weathering of time and of stone removal for building elsewhere. Today the site is well worth a visit, for the castle ruins and Constable's House (both looked after by English Heritage) stand in a glorious part of Christchurch – beside the beautiful River Avon and in the shadow of the town's magnificent priory.

CORFE CASTLE

Location: On the northern edge of the village of Corfe Castle, alongside the A351 between Wareham and Swanage.
OS Reference: SY 957823.
Viewing: Open to the public at the times advertised by the National Trust. 'The Rings' can be viewed from the public footpath running adjacent to them.

With its eight towers, two gatehouses, massive keep and other buildings, there is probably no more famous or historic a ruin in the whole of the British Isles than Corfe Castle. It is as magnificent when seen from within its bailey as it is when glimpsed from afar, projecting skywards in a natural gap in the Purbeck Hills.

Located within a natural moat formed by two streams, there was already a royal palace at Corfe prior to the reign of William the Conqueror, but it is to the Conqueror that we owe the origins of the great royal castle that remains today. Like most medieval castles, Corfe's evolution was a gradual process. A succession of monarchs added to or improved its design. For example, the main keep was not added until 1105, the middle bailey was completed in about 1240 and the outer bailey some 40 years later. Near the keep stand the remains of the Gloriette, a much more domestic royal residence built in the early thirteenth century for King John, who regularly stayed in the castle whilst hunting in the Isle of Purbeck.

William I worked on a building which had already seen regal intrigue and mystery, for it was whilst staying at Corfe with his stepmother Elfrida, that King Edward the Martyr was assassinated in 978 – some say by poisoning and others by being dragged from his

Two engravings of Corfe Castle. The first, of 1643, shows the castle under
siege by Parliament during the Civil War. The second one, of 1660 –
the year of the Restoration of the Monarchy, is of the ruins that
remained after the castle was demolished in 1646.

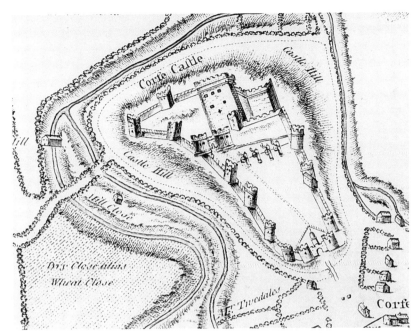

A detail from Ralph Treswell's survey of Corfe Castle in 1585.

horse and killed by her bodyguards – thereby allowing Elfrida's natural son Ethelred (the 'Unready') to mount the English throne.

During its history the castle was besieged on four occasions, the first two being during the reign of King Stephen – of which little is recorded, save for the fact that both were unsuccessful. Over the next half a millennium, with stone outer walls replacing the original timber palisades, Corfe served successively as a royal residence, as a military fortress with a resident garrison and as a grand family home. In 1635 Sir John Bankes bought the castle from the crown, and it was whilst in Oxford with Charles I that eight years later, during the Civil War, his wife, Lady Mary, led the resistance against the attacking Roundhead forces. By 1643 Corfe was almost alone in the whole of Dorset in still being in the hands of the Royalists and, with only a garrison of five men and her maids, the gallant lady and her volunteers held out for some six weeks until the Parliamentary force admitted defeat and withdrew their seige engines.

An aerial photograph of Corfe Castle from the north-east.
The keep of 1105 stands in the centre of the ruins.
Previous page Corfe Castle.

In 1644 Sir John Bankes died whilst still in Oxford, so it was on Lady Bankes's shoulders that the mantle of responsibility fell when in 1646 elements of Fairfax's New Model Army again attempted to force Corfe Castle into submission. Once again the defenders withstood the siege, and it was only through the treachery of a member of the garrison, Lieutenant Colonel Pitman, who let Parliamentary troops from Weymouth and Lulworth Castle into the castle under the guise of bringing in reinforcements, that the surrender of the castle and the overthrow of its defenders was finally achieved.

In March 1646 the House of Commons voted for the castle to be demolished – the result being the picturesque ruins that we see at Corfe today – and in 1981 the Bankes family bequeathed the site to the National Trust, who continue to care for it in the Trust's usual exemplary manner. At the Visitor Centre, on the north side of Corfe Castle village, there is an excellent presentation on the castle's history. To enjoy your visit, and appreciate the castle's history and development, it is well worthwhile calling here first.

CORFE CASTLE RINGS. Some 330 yards (300 m) to the south-west of the main castle (at SY 955820), between the River Corfe and the road leading to Steeple and the Purbeck Hills – on the only large enough flat area adjacent to the main castle for a besieging force to form up and deploy – stand the earthwork remains of a 'Ring and Bailey' castle. It covers just over two acres and consists of a substantial bank, in the form of a circular enclosure, and an external ditch. These are the remains of a medieval siege works built in 1139 when King Stephen's forces unsuccessfully laid seige to the main castle, and were used again during the Civil War as the site of a Cromwellian gun battery.

Location: Alongside an unclassified road a short distance to the south-east of Cranborne village.

OS Reference: SU 059127.

Viewing: From the public footpath which runs below the bailey of the castle on its northern side.

Some half a mile from Cranborne village (not to be confused with Cranborne Manor, a former hunting lodge in the heart of the village, originally built by King John) stood Cranborne Castle, a motte and bailey castle located on a 200 feet (61 m) high ridge, known as Castle Hill, overlooking the valley of the River Crane.

It is probable that the crown was responsible for its construction, for Cranborne was then a royal manor, and the new castle would have also stood guard over the main road between Salisbury and south Dorset. The castle's earthworks covered approximately 2½ acres, with the motte being some 180 feet (55 m) across, with a 25 feet (7.6 m) high ditch fortifying the west and north-west sides and a crescent shaped bailey to the east, itself bounded by a high rampart and outer ditch. Entrance to the castle seems to have been via a causeway approaching the bailey from the south, and it is likely that there was no significant masonry work at the site, the defensive structures being made from local timbers.

Today, because the area is heavily overgrown, it is hard to appreciate the layout of the castle in its functional· days. However, a visit does make one aware of how the motte and bailey lay relative to each other and of the size of the bailey wall (which is still very well preserved). The bluebells, bracken and bird life here in spring and early summer are delightful but, as most of the growth is deciduous, Cranborne Castle is best visited on a crisp winter's day.

Location: On the north side of Dorchester, where Dorchester Prison now stands.

OS Reference: SY 693909.

Viewing: The site is best viewed from the footpaths running through meadows of the Frome Valley directly north of the Prison.

The first purpose-built castle in the county town of Dorchester was probably the one started in 1070 for use by the forces of William the Conqueror, although such an important and strategic town already possessed the walls which had once surrounded the Roman town. The castle was built just inside the line of these walls.

In medieval times Dorchester Castle stood in the northern part of the town. We know that it possessed a fine hall with Portesham stone pillars and that the defensive ditch was dug where Glyde Path Road and Colliton Street run today, but there are no records of its shape or design. Some records do though exist of expenditure on the castle: 1202 – 'Repairs to our Castle at Dorcestre (*sic*) – 50 shillings'; 1209 – 'Cost of keeping King's horses at Dorchester – 65s 3d'.

King John was a regular visitor to Dorchester and stayed in the castle eleven times between 1201 and 1204. On leaving at the end of his final visit he is reputed to have taken with him the jewels and fineries that had previously been stored in its vault. It seems that the castle passed out of royal ownership between 1290 and 1309, but contemporary records are unclear.

For most of its history the castle was probably only lightly armed and of relatively minor military significance, a fact emphasised by the moving of the County Jail (from a site near the present White Hart public house) to Castle Hill in 1745 and the building of a new jail there from 1790 to 1794. This entailed the removal of all the remains of the castle standing above ground.

In 1720, during construction of a Presbyterian Meeting House on Castle Hill, one large and two small cavities were discovered in the chalk which were possibly subterranean passages linking castle and town. Further excavations at the prison site in 1975 uncovered evidence of the former occupancy:: the massive ditch was encountered as was a possible Civil War curved ditch.

POUNDBURY BARRACKS. Dorchester does possess one fort-like building which merits inclusion: the remaining keep at the Poundbury Barracks (also known as Depot Barracks) at the western end of the town's High Street (SY 688907). When the Dorset Volunteer Rangers (later the Queen's Own Dorset Yeomanry) was raised in 1794 what later became known as the Marabout Barracks was built on a neighbouring site as its base. It consisted of a central block and two detached wings, of which the central block and north wing remain. What also remains, behind the Keep, are most of the Victorian buildings of the Barracks square.

The impressive keep was erected in 1879 as an armourer's stores and was designed to be defensible – hence the firing ports and original strong gates. It now serves as the Military Museum of Devon and Dorset, and is open daily from 9.30 am to 5.00 pm (plus Bank Holiday Sundays).

The keep at the Poundbury Barracks in Dorchester.

[24]

Location: Astride the minor road running due south from East Chelborough village.

OS Reference: ST 552054 (Castle Hill) and ST 554055 (Stake Farm).

Viewing: From the road between the sites, although it is difficult to see much at all of the Stake Farm site without permission of the landowner.

There are two medieval castle sites at East Chelborough, probably of similar vintage, although it is unlikely that they both were in use at the same time. They are known locally as the Castle Hill and the Stake Farm Castles.

There appears to be no obvious explanation today as to why one, let alone two, castles were built here – save that there are indications that there was a deer park in this part of Dorset and that a local landowner exercised his hunting rights in the area. It is possible that the castle at Stake Farm was built first and, being low lying, found to be too damp and abandoned in favour of the second site. Equally, it is just conceivable that the smaller structure was a 'siege castle', although this seems unlikely as its lower elevation placed it at a disadvantage to defenders on Castle Hill. A third theory is that Stake Farm Castle was not fully defendable, and that its residents could take refuge on Castle Hill when danger threatened. No records exist of either castle seeing action; nor are there any documenting their gradual disintegration. Unless some future archaeological dig comes up with a particularly relevant find we shall probably never have an answer to this conundrum.

The more impressive of the two sets of remains is that on Castle Hill, where the defensive structure crowned the summit of a 600 feet (183 m) high hill. It consisted of an irregular shaped bailey with an oval-shaped motte some 30 feet (9 m) high in its south-west corner – which may owe its height to artificial steepening of the natural contours of the hill. Unlike the other rural castles in West Dorset – Chideock, Marshwood and Powerstock – Castle Hill is clearly visible from some distance away, allowing the modern visitor to appreciate

This early post-war aerial view of East Chelborough's Castle Hill shows the impressive earthworks that remain at the site of the former medieval fort. The panorama is little altered today.

how strategically positioned was the site chosen by its medieval builders (the best view is from the *cul-de-sac* leading down to the neighbouring village of West Chelborough). There is a trig point marker on the former motte – now, in itself, an item of historical value as map and chart making moves on to satellite positioning technology!

Some 150 yards (137 m) to the north-east of the Castle Hill site, much damaged by time and the plough, is the site of the other East Chelborough castle, Stake Farm Castle. This smaller structure consisted of a simple motte and bailey, of which very little remains – just a rise of some 12 feet (3.6 m) or so where the motte stood and a defensive bank running north-south some 100 yards (90 m) or so to its east. It is even possible that this defensive bank is, in fact, nothing more than natural contouring of the ground.

Location: East Lulworth, alongside the B3070 from Lulworth Cove to Wareham.

OS Reference: SY 855821.

Viewing: Good views from the footpath through the park along the south side of the building; entry at the times advertised by English Heritage.

The area of land on which Lulworth Castle now stands was first built on in the thirteenth century, when the de Newburgh family built its manor house, but it was Thomas, 3rd Lord Howard of Bindon, who probably began the construction of the present castle in 1608. The castle was not specifically built for defence alone, but was designed both to entertain and to impress, with its main *raison d'être* being as

Masking the fact that much of its interior is an empty void, Lulworth Castle today displays an impressive exterior. The prominent classical arch and the statues at the head of the staircase were eighteenth century additions to the facade.

a grand hunting lodge – a lodge grand enough to be much enjoyed by James I when hunting in the Purbecks. The castle is of considerable interest, though its architect is not known. With a round tower at each corner and a complementary central square tower, it was surrounded by landscaped gardens and a deer park.

The Weld family, still the current owners, acquired Lulworth Castle in 1641, only to have to hand it over to Charles I's forces one year later to house a Royalist garrison on the outbreak of the Civil War. Three years after this it was lost to Parliament and, although it had played no major role in the war, as a reprisal for the loyalty shown by the Welds to the crown, it was stripped bare of all its valuables and fittings.

With the Restoration of the Monarchy in 1660, Humphrey Weld was able to return to his beloved Dorset and set about restoring the castle to its former glory. Subsequently the castle was modernised a number of times in line with current contemporary fashion, only to fall victim to an uncontrollable fire in August 1929. The outbreak is thought to have started in the north-east tower, probably due to an electrical fault, and gutted the entire building – although many of the family heirlooms were saved.

Empty, and left to face the elements for more than half a century, Lulworth Castle is now managed by English Heritage who, in conjunction with the Weld Estate and in preference to stabilising the castle as a picturesque ruin, are restoring the external appearance of the building. This is a major undertaking, as the stonework has a high chalk content and is in a fragile condition, but glazed windows have been reinstalled, the central tower has been rebuilt and roofed and a spiral staircase has been installed in the south-east tower. The climb of its 136 steps will reward you with marvellous views of Poole Harbour, the English Channel (through Arish Mell Gap) and the Purbeck Hills.

Location: In open countryside at Lodge House Farm, some 2 miles to the south east of the village of Marshwood.

OS Reference: SY 405977.

Viewing: No access. The bulk of the ruins can be seen from the public footpath passing north-south through the adjacent farmyard.

This castle, together with the adjacent St Mary's Chapel, was built at the beginning of the thirteenth century by William de Mandeville, Baron of Marshwood. The rectangular keep stands on a motte in the south-west corner of defensive earthworks, surrounded by an almost square-shaped moat. The keep was approximately 40 feet x 30 feet (14.5 m x 9.1 m), and consisted of stone and rubble walls some 10 feet (3 m) thick.

Historical references to Marshwood Castle are few and far between. It is known that Baron Robert Mandeville was on the

The small surviving portion of Marshwood Castle.

Viewed looking north, this aerial view of Marshwood Castle
clearly shows the remaining sections of the moat.

victorious barons' side against Henry III and his son Edward I at the Battle of Lewes (1264), but later received a royal pardon when the fortunes of the loyalists were restored. The pardon saved Mandeville's life, but not his tenure of the barony, and from this time onwards Marshwood Castle slowly declined in importance: land was sold off and little attempt made to keep the stone or earthworks in a meaningful state of repair. By the time of the Civil War, the castle would have been of no military importance. No records exist of it seeing combat during the conflict, and it is probable that no effort was made to check its decline into the state we see it in today.

Some stonework still remains, together with a small amount of low-level earthworks to the north of the motte and the residue of the moat to the south-west. Although there is no access to the castle itself, good views can be obtained from the footpath which passes between the castle and Lodge House Farm.

POWERSTOCK CASTLE

Location: To the south of the unclassified road leading from Powerstock eastward to Whetley and Powerstock Common.
OS Reference: SY 522958.
Viewing: A number of public footpaths from both Powerstock and Nettlecombe lead directly to the castle earthworks, to which there is virtually unrestricted access.

Local, and probably misplaced, tradition has it that 'Porstock' castle was the winter palace of the Saxon King Athelstan – grandson of Alfred the Great and King of Wessex from 925 to 940. But if such a palace did exist, all traces of it have since vanished (although evidence has been uncovered of a possible Celtic encampment on the site).

In reality, the castle at Powerstock was first started in 1205, either as a brand new building or as a major rebuilding of an already existing manor house. In September 1205 King John exchanged some of the land in his manor in Fordington for land in the manor of Porstock, with Nettlecombe and Stafford. The King had actually had his eye on the site for some while, for two years earlier he had ordered building materials to be delivered to the village.

The castle was a motte-and-bailey earthwork occupying a roughly triangular promontory of some 9 acres, with the motte to the north and a kidney-shaped bailey to the south, with an outer enclosure surrounding the rest of the promontory. Although its existence allowed the king to use it as a base from which to collect tolls from merchants and travellers using the route between Dorchester, Bridport and Lyme Regis, he mainly used it as a hunting lodge. William of Montacute was ordered to 'guard the woods well' as they were extensively stocked with game, and the king's last visit was in 1213, three years before his death. It remained in royal ownership, but little used, until 1266, when Henry III granted it to Sir Ralph de Gorges. Sir Ralph much preferred his Bradpole mansion and let the castle fall into disrepair. Much of the stone was incorporated into houses in Powerstock, but two hundred years ago several sections of stonework were still standing, for the eighteenth century historian John Hutchins reported '*several vaults of stone remaining and some of the walls standing*'. There is now not a fragment of masonry to be seen, for much of the ruins were long ago quarried to supply a nearby lime kiln.

From the top of the former motte the modern visitor can enjoy far-reaching views in all directions (particularly towards the massive hillfort at Eggardon) and the nearer panorama of the beautiful villages of Powerstock and Nettlecombe nestling in the valley below.

RUFUS (BOW AND ARROW) CASTLE

Location: Above Church Ope Cove, Portland – adjacent to Portland Museum.
OS Reference: SY 697712.
Viewing: Currently no public access; readily seen from adjacent public footpaths.

Known equally well locally as Rufus Castle or as Bow and Arrow Castle, the present set of ruins stand on a single pinnacle of rock on the cliffs above Church Ope Cove and Penn Wears and, at the very least, are the remains of the second castle to have been built on the same site.

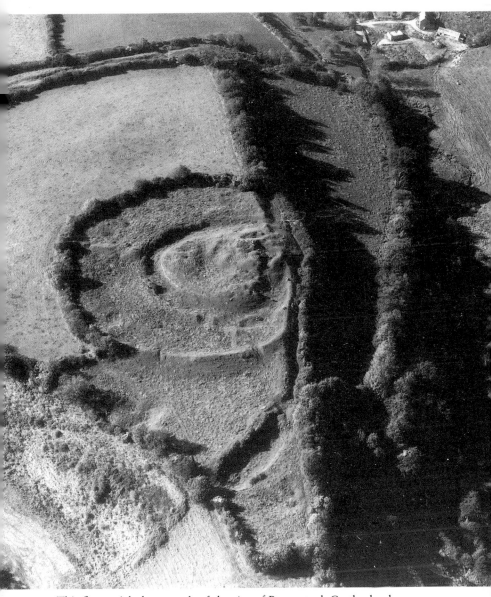

This fine aerial photograph of the site of Powerstock Castle clearly
shows the inner motte and outer bailey. To the north (the right) the
motte is defended by the ground falling away, on the other sides
by a semi-circular ditch.

The nomenclature of the castle leads to confusion: the firing positions within the stoneworks, the splayed embrasures, are definitely gunports and not designed for use by archers, whilst the ruins themselves date from a later era than the days of William II – 'King Rufus'.

There was certainly a castle here in 1142, for records reveal that it was then taken from King Stephen and ceded as a gift to Empress Maud by Robert, Duke of Gloucester. Later records are sparse, the only recorded keeper being Richard de Clare, Duke of Gloucester, whose stewardship was during the reign of Henry III and to whom permission was given to crenellate the building in 1258. The castle he built, probably on the same site as William II's defence works, provided the foundations for the present keep or blockhouse, built by Richard, Duke of York during the mid-fifteenth century.

'Blockhouse' is an apt description, as there was probably never an outer defensive wall, and it is quite possible that the castle was never

Above A rarely seen view of the interior of Rufus Castle, showing the shape of the splayed embrasures and their unsuitability for use by archers. *Opposite page* Rufus Castle, Portland, with the ruins of the medieval church of St Andrew in the foreground.

completed as originally designed. However, the fact that there is no well within the present structure indicates that some additional land around the keep must have been fortified to meet this most basic of defensive military necessities.

What we see today are the remains of a three storey, pentagon-shaped keep, built of Portland stone with very little mortar, with walls up to 7 feet (2.1 m) thick, and with no firing positions on the side next to the cliff edge. The original access to the building was from the south-west corner. The bridge to the north of the castle, crossing over the pathway to Church Ope is a later addition. Both the bridge, and the mock-Norman archway adjacent to it, were added by John Penn when Governor of Portland during the late eighteenth and early nineteenth centuries.

The passage of time has not been kind to Rufus Castle. Coastal erosion and the removal of stone for building purposes have reduced the site to a mere classical ruin. However, English Heritage (in co-operation with the present owner, a Dorset stonemason) does have plans to make the building safe enough to admit visitors once more. Meanwhile – even in its present state – it is well worth a visit and is equally attractive when viewed from the adjacent footpath, the beach below or from the nearby ruins of St Andrew's Church.

SHAFTESBURY CASTLE

Location: The north-west corner of the town of Shaftesbury.
OS Reference: ST 857228.
Viewing: There is unrestricted access. Follow the signs to 'Castle Hill' or 'Hill', and the earthworks are to be found just beyond the kissing gate on the edge of the park in the street named Bimport. Good views can also be obtained from Breach Lane which, at the bottom of Tout Hill, runs below the site.

Although early Shaftesbury was more famous for the abbey which King Alfred ordered to be built than its castle, it is known that the king used the town as one of the bases from which he mounted his successful ninth century campaigns against the invading Danes. However, archaeological surveys between 1947 and 1949 only uncovered

Shaftesbury from the south-west. The town sits on a greensand spur 700 feet above sea level, and is protected on three sides by the fall of the land. The castle's earthworks are contained within the triangular piece of ground at the tip of the spur in the foreground (in front of the now demolished gas holder). The town promenade, Park Walk, is clearly visible on the right.

evidence of occupation of the site during the twelfth and thirteenth centuries. Notably the excavations uncovered no Iron Age, Roman or late medieval remains – the most interesting find being a cut halfpenny coin from the reign of King Stephen.

The castle, of which no plan remains, stood on a sharp, steep promontory to the west of the plateau upon which the town of Shaftesbury stands, and was protected from the east by a deep, artificial ditch. A deep pit, known locally as Cobbler's Pit (and still easily spotted), possibly marks the site of a free standing defensive tower, and it seems likely that Shaftesbury Castle was probably only a temporary defensive structure with a limited lifespan.

Today the site is overgrown and has been much altered by man since its military days. The casual observer could be excused for failing to appreciate the significance of the site if not forewarned of its presence, although the steep western face of the site has an obvious fortification connection. There are extensive views deep into Wiltshire, with equally rewarding views south into Dorset from the town's war memorial, just a few hundred yards away from the former castle.

SHERBORNE (OLD) CASTLE

Location: At the end of Castleton Road, on the north shore of Sherborne Lake.
OS Reference: ST 653167.
Viewing: The castle is open to the public.

Known as the 'old' castle to distinguish it from the nearby Sherborne (New) Castle, which was never a true castle but a compact family home designed for Sir Walter Raleigh, Sherborne Old Castle stands in an elevated and commanding position on the north side of Sherborne Lake, within what is today called Sherborne Park. Although only slightly south of the town of Sherborne, it lies within the parish of Castleton, and archaeological excavations indicate pre-Norman occupation of the site.

The castle whose ruins we see today was once of major importance, serving as a seat of power for both church and crown. It was

An aerial photograph of Sherborne Old Castle from the north. Note the
secondary keep outside the moat on the west (the right), with the gatehouse
in the south-western corner.

A late eighteenth century engraving of Sherborne Old Castle. Two centuries later, the view from this vantage point remains remarkably similar.

originally built by Roger de Caen, an unscrupulous medieval official who combined spiritual office with secular power. He was appointed Chancellor of England when Henry I became king in 1100, and shortly afterwards was created Bishop of Salisbury – a diocese that included Sherborne. As well as building Sherborne castle, he also built castles at Old Sarum, Devizes and Malmesbury. After Henry's death in 1135, Roger de Caen fell from favour. His castles were confiscated by the crown, and he ended his days disgraced and broken.

Its central buildings were built around a cloistered courtyard; there were certainly four towers (possibly more during the reign of Edward III) and a barbican and external wall, with a secondary keep to the west. Much of the main, internal keep is still standing, but the only tower still remaining at any height is that which stood in the south-west corner – by which access is gained today.

During the period of relative calm that prevailed over southern England for the next 300 years or so, Sherborne Castle passed through the hands of a succession of owners, with Elizabeth I obtaining a 99 year lease on the property in 1591. A year later she transferred it to Sir Walter Raleigh, who had wanted the castle since seeing it on his journeys between London and Devon. He attempted to convert the castle into a domestic residence, and his various alterations were instrumental in reducing its fighting effectiveness. The results were never very satisfactory and, whilst still maintaining the original structure in its reduced form, he decided instead to build a lodge house to the south of the castle which has been greatly expanded over the years into the much grander Sherborne (New) Castle. During the building of the new property, the original castle was used as a barracks for some 500 troops, a sign of the importance and esteem in which Sir Walter was held by the crown.

Some half a century after Raleigh had tampered with its defences, the castle was to be put to the ultimate military test for the first time. As a symbol of all that Oliver Cromwell thought wrong with Royalist England, Sherborne Castle was first attacked by Parliamentarian forces in 1642. William Seymour, 1st Marquess of Hertford, who had retreated to Sherborne from Wells with 500 cavalry and reinforced the castle defences, then in a state of disrepair, successfully fought off this seige. However, in August 1645 the Royalist defenders commanded by Sir Lewis Dyve, the Governor, were not so successful. After a 15 day seige the forces of General Thomas Fairfax, under the cover of a series of massive artillery bombardments, breached the defences and overthrew the garrison. The lives of the garrison were spared, but all the goods and chattels seized from the castle were sold off the next day at Sherborne market.

Almost immediately the order was given to reduce the castle to ruins and it was this action, together with the ravages of the passing of time and the denuding of the stonework to provide building materials, that has led to the original Sherborne Castle becoming the dramatic ruin we see today.

Visible across the lake to the south is Sherborne (New) Castle. This property – a turreted house and not a true castle – is now in the possession of the famous Dorset Digby family, although they are no longer in residence. The original lodge from Sir Walter Raleigh's days has greatly been expanded upon, with four castellated wings added in 'H' form. Under the stewardship of English Heritage, it is open to the public at well-advertised times and, although externally rather unattractive, is well worth viewing for its connections with Sir Walter Raleigh.

STURMINSTER NEWTON CASTLE

Location: Alongside the A357 road, immediately south of Sturminster Newton bridge.
OS Reference: ST 785134.
Viewing: It is possible to see clearly the general area of the site, but only to obtain glimpses the ruins, from the footpath which runs to the west of the site (signposted, opposite the bridge, 'To Hole House Lane'). The best views will be in winter, at which time the normally dense foliage will be reduced.

On a site where an Iron Age fort covering some 4 acres or so once stood and where the West Saxon kings held court, Sturminster Newton Castle occupied a commanding position on a steep-sided spur immediately above the crossing of the River Stour, which led off the route between the important trading centres of Blandford Forum and Sherborne into the town itself.

Although even today it is possible to appreciate the extensive ground contouring which must have taken place here – including the digging of a crescent-shaped ditch some 350 feet (107 m) long and up to 40 feet (12 m) wide – it is not known when the castle was constructed or, indeed, what overall shape and form it took. It is, however, recorded that King John had the castle provisioned in 1208 and that heavy fighting here during the War of the Roses led to its destruction. We know that by 1529 no significant part of the structure remained standing, although as late as 1890 repairs to the 'last arch of the old castle' were carried out by General Pitt-Rivers, a local landowner and the 'father' of modern archaeology.

After the Dissolution of the Monasteries, the manor of Sturminster passed to the Crown and was granted in 1544 to Queen Katherine

The attractive manor house ruins which stand adjacent to the
original site of Sturminster Newton Castle.

Parr – who erected a fine manor house in the grounds of the former
castle, probably slightly to the north of the original building. Thus
the ruins which the visitor sees today are not castle ruins, but those
of a large manor house, possibly not the original one built by
Katherine but a replacement constructed post-1630. The site is well
looked after, the grass being kept cut and the whole area neat and
tidy. A polite request at nearby Castle Farm may even allow you
access.

Location: Within the town walls, between Pound Lane and the River Frome.

OS Reference: SY 922872.

Viewing: None, except for an arch and some stonework removed to Pound Lane.

Nestling behind earthwork walls of indeterminate ancient times (possibly pre-Roman Conquest), Wareham – once the largest town in Dorset and an important port on the River Frome – formerly boasted a castle with a keep larger than that at nearby Corfe. Now only the motte upon which it stood remains and, save for a small amount of reclaimed stonework and an arch from Norman times in Pond Lane, all else has long since disappeared.

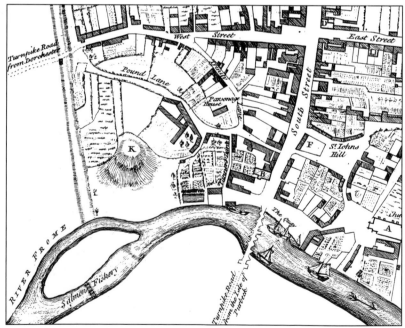

A detail from a plan of Wareham from Hutchins' *History of Dorset* (1774) showing the site of the former castle (marked with the letter 'K').

John Hutchins remains Dorset's greatest historian, and it is perhaps apt that
the only surviving pieces from Wareham Castle, this recovered stonework
and part of a Norman arch, should be set in the wall
of his former parsonage in Pound Lane.

The castle stood in the south-west corner of the town, adjacent
to where earlier Roman and Saxon defensive structures had been
destroyed by the Danes in 876. It overlooked the River Frome, which
in medieval times was sufficiently wide and deep for large sea-going
ships to sail up-river to Wareham. The castle was built by William
the Conqueror between 1086 and about 1100 on land on which a
number of dwellings are known to have been demolished to make
way for it.

The keep was square, with walls some 13 feet (4 m) thick, and the top of the motte had a diameter of 120 feet (36.6 m), but we know nothing about any further buildings or details of the bailey. The castle changed hands many times during the wars between King Stephen and the Empress Maud and, although badly damaged, was still considered worthy of garrisoning in 1216 when King John reinforced it as a precaution against attack from France. Thereafter, with the castle at Corfe enjoying a considerably better defensive location, Wareham Castle was slowly allowed to fall into disrepair. Edward I was the last reigning monarch to visit the castle and by the middle of the fifteenth century it was in use as a private garden, although still in royal ownership.

The site has seen many other changes of ownership over the last 500 years or so, and today the unusually named house 'Castle Close', nestling behind high walls and an impressive gateway, stands where this once important castle once stood. To the south-west of the former motte a substantive amount of the old ditch, some 22 feet (6.7 m) deep and 70 feet (21.3 m) across, remains. Nearby in Pound Lane, in the wall of the former rectory where the Reverend John Hutchins (1698–1773) compiled his monumental *The History and Antiquities of Dorset*, are the only remaining above ground traces of the castle – recovered stonework and a small Norman archway. Archaeological excavations in 1952 and 1953 charted the remaining foundations of both the keep and parts of the bailey – now some 15 feet (4.6 m) below ground level and, in part, beneath the present house.

WOODSFORD CASTLE

Location: Adjacent to the village of the same name, on the minor road running from West Stafford to Moreton.
OS Reference: SY 758904.
Viewing: Access restricted to those staying there with the Landmark Trust, but can be admired from the adjacent highway.

On a site chronicled in the Doomsday Survey of 1086 as possessing a manor or small estate, Woodsford Castle stands sentinel beside a major ford across the River Frome. The castle was either erected, or vastly improved upon, by Sir Guy de Bryene, a close friend of Edward III, who acquired the manor and bailiwick here in 1367 and was granted permission by the king to 'crenellate the dwelling house of his manor'. The importance of this particular crossing of the Frome was evidenced by the beacon which was burnt at night on top of the castle's north-east tower to mark its location, but it is most likely that the fortifying of the house was as a response to local unrest – coastal raiding, for example – rather than because of the importance of the ford.

No records exist of the exact early form of the castle, although it is said to have been similar to the slightly later Chideock Castle, which was started in 1380. We do know, however, that it was a long rectangular building of Purbeck limestone and aligned along a north/south axis with a courtyard to its west, and that it once possessed 5 defensive towers – one on each corner with the fifth centrally on the east wall adjacent to the castle guardroom. There was perhaps also a gatehouse, most probably in the west wall. With defence in mind, the castle was laid out in such a way that all the residential accommodation was above ground floor level and accessible only through a guardroom at the top of a narrow and winding staircase. As built, there were no doors or large windows on the ground floor.

The west front of Woodsford Castle, showing the two sets
of steps leading up the first floor entrances.

By 1630 the castle had fallen into disrepair, and it was after this that the original roof was replaced by thatch, making Woodsford Castle the largest thatched manor house in Dorset and the only thatched castle throughout the realm. Another major restoration project started in 1850 (under the supervision of Thomas Hardy's father), and together these two rebuilds altered the emphasis on Woodsford's use from defensive to simply residential, with the property becoming merely a large farmhouse, whose ground floor rooms were used to pen livestock. Today only the north-east tower remains intact and the walls of the courtyard no longer stand, although the outline of where the wall joined the main building in its south-east corner is still clearly visible.

In 1978 the Landmark Trust bought the castle, later undertaking the third major restoration in the castle's history. It is now one of over 200 historically interesting buildings in the Trust's ownership and is available for rent as a holiday home. Your chance to live in a castle!

As a reminder of how defensive philosophies have changed over the years, it is interesting to note, standing in the castle's grounds today, a pillbox from the Second World War – sited, as was its fourteenth century predecessor, to cover the crossing over the River Frome.

THE TUDOR PERIOD

The castles and forts built during the sixteenth century are often referred to as 'Henrician', a name they owe to Henry VIII as it was he who provided the initial impetus for their construction. They were developments of the medieval castle, but their defensive strength against an overseas invader was central to their design and layout. Less grand than their Norman predecessors, and sited to fill a specific and different role, they still retained features which made it possible to resist attack from land as well as from naval forces.

The Reformation, and Pope Clement VII's refusal in 1534 to grant Henry VIII a divorce, had led to a sharp deterioration of his relationship with the papacy and the Catholic continental powers, most especially France and the Holy Roman Empire. Fearing a possible invasion across the Channel, and despite having the most efficient navy the country had ever possessed, Henry ordered a survey of the potentially threatened south and east coasts. The survey extended from Pembrokeshire to Berwick-upon-Tweed, and its aim was to identify places vulnerable to attack and to plan how best to defend them.

Dorset's leading commissioner for the project was John Russell, 1st Duke of Bedford, who had been born at Kingston Russell. He surveyed the coast in the spring of 1539, proposing works of various kinds at Bournemouth, Poole, Brownsea, Portland, the Nothe at Weymouth, Sandsfoot, and at the end of the Cobb at Lyme Regis. His proposals, even if accepted in principle, were never fully carried out: the forts at Bournemouth, Poole and Lyme were never built, whilst that at Brownsea was built by the Poole burgesses and was never a royal castle.

The principal armament of this new generation of forts was sited within the castle's casemates, but secondary batteries were often provided on external platforms. The disadvantage of the casemate guns was the masking of the target by trapped gun smoke, whilst the outside positions left the gunners more exposed to return fire.

Of the three Henrician forts on the Dorset coast, Portland and Sandsfoot were placed to have overlapping arcs of fire across Portland and Weymouth Roads, whilst Brownsea covered the approaches to Poole Harbour. It was these castles, updated in detail only, which saw action during the Civil War, prepared for combat during the time of the Spanish Armada and the Napoleonic Wars and remained supreme until the building of their replacements in the late nineteenth century.

BROWNSEA (BRANKSEA) CASTLE

Location: Brownsea Island, at the entrance to Poole Harbour.
OS Reference: SZ 029876.
Viewing: The castle is now in private ownership, but clear views can be seen – most especially from boats approaching the Island. Access to the Island is by means of pleasure cruisers from Poole Quay and Sandbanks.

Brownsea Castle (known also until 1903 as Branksea) stands on the eastern shores of Brownsea Island adjacent to the landing quay. It began life as a blockhouse built between 1545 and 1547 to serve as Poole Harbour's primary defensive bastion against marauding French warships. Money for its construction, fitting out and arming came mainly from the merchants of Poole who, as well as obeying formal directives to meet this public obligation, were eager to protect both the town and their shipping.

The original building was single storey, with a moat around the three landward sides and with its main gun platform facing out across the deep water channel between the Sandbanks and Studland Peninsulas. As such, it was more a protected garrison building than a fort capable of providing meaningful all round defence. In later years its height was raised to give greater protection against possible incoming fire from adjacent higher ground, but all that remains of the original Tudor castle are the stone walls in what is now the basement.

A map of Poole Harbour of 1597 highlighting the strategic importance
of Brownsea Island at the Harbour entrance. The map is of great
interest in that it shows the only known floor plan and drawing
of the Tudor blockhouse.

During the Civil War it was upgraded and garrisoned by Parliamentary forces but never tested in combat. Eventually ownership
of the island passed to the Sturt family, and in 1786 the Bridport
MP Charles Sturt inherited the estate and set about converting the
blockhouse into a fine family home. The resultant expansion saw
Brownsea blessed with a square tower block four storeys high, set
symmetrically within four built-up wings and complemented to the
north by a turreted enclosure, with expansion on a lesser scale con-
tinuing well into the nineteenth century.

In January 1896, as the family of the then owner Kenneth Balfour
MP were at evensong in the Island's church, fire swept through the
now gothic-like structure and destroyed most of its contents. The
subsequent restoration and rebuilding did away with some of the
more extreme embellishments and left Brownsea Castle in very much
the state that we see it today – no longer a fortified mansion, but

Brownsea Castle seen from Poole Harbour today. The Family Pier to the right, with its two stucco-faced watch towers in the Tudor style, was built by Colonel Waugh in the 1850s.

merely an extremely attractive large house set in an idyllic location.

During the Second World War Brownsea's military connections were restored, for a pair of former naval 4.7inch guns were mounted adjacent to the castle to guard the harbour approaches – just as those of the blockhouse had done some 400 years earlier. The associated searchlight buildings are still visible, but the underground control bunker below the gun mountings – which themselves can still be seen – has been filled in.

Today Brownsea Castle is used as a recreation and conference centre for the staff of the John Lewis Partnership. The rest of this beautiful island has, since 1961, been in the ownership of the National Trust.

PORTLAND CASTLE

Location: The southern shore of Portland Harbour (clearly signposted), adjacent to the Naval Air Station.
OS Reference: SY 685744.
Viewing: Open to the public at the times advertised by English Heritage. In addition to road access, White Motor Boats run a service to the castle from Weymouth.

Portland Castle is one of the country's best preserved Henrician coastal defence castles. It was built to afford complementary fire to that from Sandsfoot Castle, two miles away, the two forts commanding the sheltered waters of Weymouth and Portland Roads. The castle was built at approximately the same time as its neighbour. It was operational by 1540 and constructed at a cost of almost £5,000. In accordance with the military views then prevalent, it was compact, rounded and squat, the shift from impressive hill top fortresses being

A late eighteenth century engraving of Portland Castle.

An aerial view of Portland Castle. The Constable's house stands
to the right, whilst, to the left, the grass area is the site of
the external gun platform.

designed, primarily, to offer less of a target to artillery fire, whilst its
circular design would have deflected cannon balls more easily than a
flat surface.

The castle was a two storey building, with gun embrasures on both
levels and on the roof; additionally, a gun platform stood to the
south-west side of the main walls. In 1588, the year of the Spanish
Armada, the castle was manned by 100 men and mounted 8 guns,
whilst records for 1623 show that the castle then mounted 5 further
guns. The Constable's House stood to the rear, all being surrounded
by a moat and outer earthworks.

The castle's defences were examined in 1576, when fears were
beginning to mount over Philip of Spain's wish to extend his

Catholic supremacy in mainland Europe to the British Isles, but despite the ensuing Armada scare of 1588 and frantic defensive activity along the Dorset coastline, it was not until the seventeenth century Civil War that the castle saw combat. It was seized by the Royalists in 1642, changed hands again twice in 1643 and finally fell to Parliamentary forces in April 1644 – following which the spoils of war collected by the victors included no less than twenty-one artillery pieces and well over a hundred muskets.

Experiencing periods of both poor and good maintenance in the years that followed, but always retaining some military significance, the castle was granted to Charles Manning early in the 1800s, whose family restored and maintained it in excellent condition until they returned it to Government ownership in 1870.

During the twentieth century it served the Royal Navy in a variety of ways, particularly as officers' accommodation and as an ammunition store, but in 1984 – save for the Constable's House, which is in private ownership – responsibility for the upkeep passed to English Heritage, who continue to maintain it in excellent condition.

Portland Castle is open to the public during the summer months – from approximately mid-March to the end of October. Full details from English Heritage on 01305 – 820539.

SANDSFOOT CASTLE

Location: In Sandsfoot Gardens, Old Castle Road, Weymouth.
OS Reference: SY 675773.
Viewing: No public access; good, close views from the gardens.

The castle at Sandsfoot, on the outskirts of the Weymouth suburb of Wyke Regis and located within the nineteenth century breakwater arms of Portland harbour, dates back to 1539. It had two principal purposes; to protect English shipping sheltering off Weymouth and Portland from foreign raiders, and to prevent an invading landing force from forming-up offshore. It is just possible that some of the stone came from Bindon Abbey, near Wool (SY 854867), which had fallen victim to Henry VIII's Dissolution of the Monasteries earlier in the year.

Two views of Sandsfoot Castle. The late eighteenth century engraving
shows the Nothe Headland in the background: the castle gateway
on the cliff edge has since fallen into the sea.
The modern photograph, taken from the outer defensive wall,
shows the precariousness of the castle's position.

The castle, of 2 storeys and dungeons, was rectangular in shape, orientated on a north-west/south-east axis and provided a heavy gun emplacement, quarters for its garrison and underground magazines. The walls were built with a variety of embrasures and loopholes to accommodate a range of different weapons, whilst the castle itself was surrounded by an encompassing ditch and a series of ramparts. Its garrison in 1588 is recorded as consisting of some 50 men.

The fortifications were surveyed in 1576, were last improved in 1623 and formally abandoned in 1665, although retained as a store until at least 1691. The royal coat of arms from the castle was saved for posterity, and is now to be found above the south entrance door at All Saints Church in nearby Wyke Regis. Being Tudor, the lion rampant is joined at the shield by a wyvern rather than the unicorn.

Designed specifically as a coastal defence, Sandsfoot Castle was always vulnerable to attack from a landward direction, and thus often changed hands during the Civil War as fortune favoured first one side and then the other. Interestingly enough, the castle dungeons are known to have been used as a mint during the Civil War – giving a greater than normal incentive to both defenders and attackers to achieve their respective aims!

Over the years the castle has gradually succumbed to coastal erosion, with the open area between its outer walls and the sea having long ago collapsed on to the beach below. Today's remains are in a dangerous state, but can be clearly seen from outside the protective fence, as can the remaining rubble on the foreshore. A fine garden has been laid out both within and without the defensive ditch's perimeter and from here the view across to the Isle of Portland, save for the intrusion of the Breakwater arms, has changed little since the days of Sandsfoot's military occupancy.

The Poisoned Cup, by Joseph Drew, is a novel of Elizabethan intrigue based upon Sandsfoot Castle. Although no longer in print, Dorset County Library has copies and it is well worth reading.

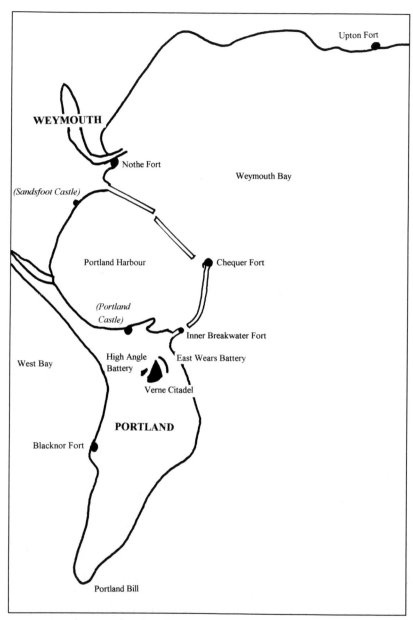

Map showing the Victorian and twentieth century forts involved in the defence of Portland Harbour and Weymouth Bay.

THE VICTORIAN FORTS

The final building phase of large Dorset fortifications was that of late Victorian times, when the coastal forts in the Weymouth and Portland areas were constructed to combat enemy shipping and assault landings. These forts differed from those which predated them in disguising their presence rather than flaunting it, and adopting a sunken profile rather than an overt one – which also served to strengthen the forts, as the gradually sloping ramparts were more resistant to gunfire than an erect wall.

Work on securing the Portland Harbour commenced in 1849, when Prince Albert laid the foundation stone, four years after Parliament first formally considered the future maritime development of the Portland area – the Inner and Outer Breakwater arms being completed in 1872. After the harbour's vulnerability to torpedo attacks was realised, the Middle and Bincleaves arms were added (1902 and 1904). To cover the harbour, major forts were built at Upton, Weymouth (Nothe Fort), on the Isle of Portland (Verne, East Wears and West Wears) and on the breakwater arms themselves.

Weaponry was advancing rapidly at the time of the building of these forts, and the muzzle-loading guns with which they were initially equipped were rapidly replaced by breech-loaders.

As late as the final years of the nineteenth century, the British Government still considered an attack from France to be the major threat to national security, but it was during the two great conflicts of the twentieth century that the forts came into their own as coastal defences and, in many cases, as anti-aircraft gun sites. During the Second World War, supplemented by innumerable pillboxes, other anti-aircraft gun sites, searchlight batteries and anti-tank obstacles, they guarded our shore during the invasion scare of 1940 and, as the fortunes of war turned in the Allies favour, stood sentinel over the forces building-up to re-occupy mainland Europe. Only in 1956,

when the Coastal Defence Regiments of the Royal Artillery were
disbanded, did the forts cease to have any further military value.

BLACKNOR (WEST WEARS) FORT

Location: High above West Bay, on the coastal footpath running
between Priory Corner and Portland Bill.
OS Reference: SY 679716.
Viewing: The property is now in private ownership; however, good
views may be had from the public rights of way to the west and south
of the fort. In addition to the approach along the coastal footpath,
there is also a way to the fort via the footpath alongside Portland
Cemetery in Weston Road.

With its commanding views across West Bay and ability to provide
enfilading fire along the sweep of Chesil Beach, Blacknor Fort stands
on the site of an earlier gun position of undefined vintage and was
completed by the contractors Jesty & Baker in 1901. Being finished

A 'between the wars' view at Blacknor Fort, with one of the fort's 9.2 inch
guns targeted across West Bay. Note that no overhead protection, either
against the weather or enemy fire, was provided for the gun crew.

that little bit later than some of its contemporaries (Chequer Fort, East Wears and the Verne Citadel) it was fitted with breech loading guns from the outset – initially of 6 inch calibre, which were later replaced by a pair of larger 9.2 inch Mk X weapons with a range of some 16 miles (25.6 km). A gun pit was provided on the north side of the fort for a 4 inch quick firing howitzer. The complement of the fort was of only 12 men – and 4 dray horses!

During the later years of the Second World War the main guns were radar-laid, though this refinement did not allow them to engage the enemy on the night of 27/28th April 1944 during the *Exercise Tiger* fiasco, as the radar plot was too confused and the risk of hitting friendly shipping instead of German E-Boats too high. (*Exercise Tiger* was an American D-Day training exercise, held in Lyme Bay and with Slapton Sands, Devon, as the task force's destination. 946 servicemen died when their landing craft were attacked by German E-boats).

Taken out of commission in 1956, Blacknor Fort is now in private ownership and is in use as cottages and a riding stables. A quick-firing gun mounting can still be seen on the footpath below the fort's protective prow.

CHEQUER (BREAKWATER) FORT

Location: On the seaward end of the Outer Breakwater Arm of Portland Harbour.
OS Reference: SY 708763.
Viewing: The fort is not accessible to the public, but it can be clearly seen from the mainland and from the many pleasure vessels cruising through Portland Harbour.

Known as the Chequer (or Chequered) Fort because of the dazzle markings around its base designed to hinder gun-ranging apparatus, Breakwater Fort provided the primary defences for military shipping taking refuge in Portland Harbour. The fort is 116 feet (35.34 m) in diameter and stands directly on the seabed, not upon a break-water arm. It was originally to be built of stone, but the plans were amended to a fort of granite with a box girder construction and armoured walls and a bombproof iron roof.

The Chequer Fort in July 1995, prior to the closure of
Portland Naval Base to surface units.

The fort became operational in 1882 with four 38 ton, 12.5 inch
muzzle loading guns. Even when first installed they were obsolete
and during the first decade of the twentieth century a major modern-
isation of the weaponry was carried out, with a Maxim machine gun,
quick firing guns and 6 inch breech loading guns being installed, all
of which were operational by 1907. The old muzzle loaders were
unceremoniously dumped over the seaward slope of the breakwater,
where they remain, readily identifiable, to this day.

The fort was manned by units of the Coastal Artillery Regiments of
the Royal Artillery and saw service during both world wars, but most
especially during the Second World War when its anti-aircraft guns
were regularly in action against German aircraft attacking shipping in

the harbour. Of interest is the fact that the vessel which supplied the fort during the 1939-45 conflict, sailing some 20,000 nautical miles and carrying over 250,000 troops and huge amounts of freight and ammunition in doing so, still plies these waters today: the *MV My Girl,* based in Weymouth Harbour and sailing from near Brewer's Quay.

Breakwater Fort was decommissioned in 1956. The fort and surrounding auxiliary buildings were tidied up before the Royal Navy surface fleet pulled out of Portland in 1995, but still present a sorry sight. Adjacent to the fort can still be seen remains of the boom defence equipment used to secure the shipping channel, together with searchlight buildings and a miscellanea of armaments such as flame throwers, depth charge launchers and anti-shipping torpedoes. The size of the garrison can be gauged by the numerous domestic and support buildings alongside.

There is a much smaller sister fort on the north eastern end of the Inner Breakwater (OS Ref: SY 703745) which was completed by 1860. Being of a less complex nature and built of Cornish granite with no armour added, it is in a much better condition; however, it saw relatively little use and during the Second World War was only fitted with a single 40mm Bofors gun.

EAST WEARS BATTERY

Location: On the slopes of steep north east cliffs of Portland between, the Verne and the Portland Young Offenders Institute.
OS Reference: SY 699731.
Viewing: Most of the complex is not currently open to the public, but the former E battery site is readily accessible via the public footpath that runs alongside the Royal Naval Cemetery (which is well signposted). The remainder of the battery sites can be clearly seen from the footpath which runs to the south of the Verne Citadel alongside the MOD security fence.

Although remote from the Verne Citadel, the East Wears Battery is actually an integral part of the Verne's defensive layout. Nevertheless, the site was independently defensible and can be considered as a

A pair of 9.2 inch breech loading guns at the East Wears battery
shortly after their installation in July 1940.

fort in its own right, even though the primary accommodation for
most of the gunners stationed here was in the main citadel and they
made for their action stations via a sally port and sheltered walkway.

There were guns positioned at East Wears certainly as far back as
1850, consisting of some 6 batteries protected by earth banks, whilst
the structures in their final form were in position by the end of the
nineteenth century. The six old battery positions (designated 1 to 6)
were replaced by just 5 new ones (A to E), with a planned armament
fit of twenty 10 inch and 9 inch muzzle loading guns – of which only
17 were actually sited.

Two particularly interesting structures remaining at East Wears are
the Defensible Barracks and the Gunners House. The Barrack building has corner bastions and loopholes to enable rifle fire to be made
from protected firing points, and was completed before the battery in
its final form became operational. The Gunners House (actually The
'Master' Gunner's residence) was completed at about the same time
and is structurally rather grand.

With the rapid advance of weapons technology during the first half
of the twentieth century numerous changes were made to the armaments. By 1939 two 9.2 inch breech loading weapons with a range of
19,700 yards (18,005 m) had replaced, and improved upon, the more
numerous guns of the late Victorian years. The E battery had a pair
of 90 mm guns mounted from 1941 until the war's end.

[64]

In common with other coastal defence positions, East Wears was deactivated in 1956, but the structures remained in use by sailors of many NATO and other friendly navies for 'fire and rescue ashore/disaster' training until Flag Officer Sea Training and his staff departed from Portland in the summer of 1995. Today the battery positions are dilapidated and, in places, overgrown – but too massive to ever likely to be completely obliterated.

FORT HENRY

Location: Redend Point, at the southern end of the beach at Studland Bay.
OS Reference: SZ 044824.
Viewing: Easily approached via the footpath through the trees above the beach.

Fort Henry is not a 'fort' in the classic sense; nevertheless it fills an important niche in the county's military history – and is certainly a 'fortified' structure.

Fort Henry, from where Winston Churchill, and Generals Eisenhower and Montgomery, watched the mock-invasion assaults of *Exercise Smash* on Studland Beach in April 1944.

The story of the American Army landing exercises off the coast of Devon prior to D-Day in the Second World War is well known, especially the tragedy of *Exercise Tiger* (see under Blacknor Fort). Less well chronicled are the similar exercises carried out on Dorset's beaches by British and Canadian troops – the *Exercise Smash* series. Thus, Fort Henry was built by Canadian engineers as a safe point from which senior officers could watch the practice landings on the Studland beaches below, with little risk of being hit by the live ammunition being used. Amongst the VIPs to view the exercise from within the bunker were Winston Churchill and Generals Montgomery and Eisenhower.

It is worth noting that by the date of Fort Henry's completion the fear of possible invasion had given way to planning a landing in mainland Europe. Thus, the fort was built in front of a defensive gun position, completely obstructing its line of fire.

NOTHE FORT

Location: Above the south side of Weymouth Harbour (well signposted).
OS Reference: SY 687787.
Viewing: Readily visible from the harbour and Nothe Gardens, the fort is open to visitors at regular times – most often during the summer months.

Defensive guns covering the approaches to Weymouth Harbour and Weymouth and Portland Roads have been sited on the headland at the Nothe since at least the mid-1550s. A small fort stood on the headland during the Civil War, but the present fort is of Victorian origin and was completed in 1872 at a cost of some £120,000. It was fitted initially with two 64 pounder, four 9 inch and six 10 inch guns – muzzle loaders with the latest state of the art spiral rifling to improve their accuracy. In the 1890s seven were replaced by massive 38 ton, 12.5 inch guns, enhancing both the fort's effective engagement range and its hitting power. At the turn of the century artillery technology was advancing rapidly, and the remaining guns were replaced with three 6 inch breech loading guns and two 6 pound

An aerial view of the Nothe Fort, showing the gun positions (both on the upper tier and, to the left, in the casemates), the outer gatehouse and defensive ditch, and - where the cars are parked - the former glacis.

quick firing guns for use against small, fast naval targets.

Other than the anti-aircraft guns positioned on the fort's glacis during the Second World War and light AA weapons, the Nothe guns, reduced from 3 to 2 in 1920, never fired a shot in anger. Indeed, except for training purposes, the only time the heavy guns fired was in July 1940 when shots were fired 'across the bows' of a pair of

The inner main entrance to the Nothe Fort, seen from the outer gatehouse beyond the defensive ditch. The restored 40 mm Bofors AA gun is one of the exhibits associated with the Museum of Coastal Defence.

unidentified passenger ships, which turned out to be carrying refugees away from German occupation of the Channel Islands!

During the war the Nothe was used as an anti-aircraft ammunition store, some of the casemates and magazines on the south (Bincleaves) side of the fort being modified for its new role.

The fort was abandoned by the Army in 1956 and the guns taken away for scrap. The local council acquired ownership in 1961 and the buildings fell into disrepair. Fortunately, the Weymouth Civic Society took over the running of the Nothe Fort in 1979, and an exceptional amount of voluntary effort has gone into turning it into today's truly excellent Museum of Coastal Defence. A visit to this impressive fortification and museum is undoubtedly of the best ways to appreciate the atmosphere of life in a Victorian fort, from both a military and a domestic point of view.

The museum is open daily during the summer months from 10.30 am to 5.30 pm; less often at other times of the year. For details telephone 01305 – 787243/786025.

One of Upton Fort's two 9.2 inch gun positions viewed from seawards.

UPTON FORT

Location: Alongside the Dorset Coast Path, half a mile to the east of the village of Osmington Mills.
OS Reference: SY 742815.
Viewing: No access; good views from adjacent public rights of way.

Upton Fort was the last of the major, static defensive positions to be built within Dorset. It was completed in 1902, as the plaque 'ER 1902' indicates, but a battery of some 4 guns is known to have been located there in the late 1880s. This older position was probably not fortified and would have consisted of muzzle-loading guns manned by the Militia.

The construction of Upton Fort was ordered to augment the fields of fire of coastal defence guns across Weymouth Bay and to complete the defence of Portland Harbour. The initial fit of guns was to be of two 6 inch and two 9.2 inch breech-loaders situated above sunken magazines, but all indications are that the smaller pair of guns never made their way to Upton and that only the 9.2 inch guns were manned during the Great War. Some of the troops based here were Australians who had been recovering from their wounds at the convalescent camps in the Weymouth area, and for whom such a posting was undoubtedly preferable to the carnage of trench warfare in Flanders.

Following the 1918 Armistice, the weaponry was removed and the fort placed on a care and maintenance footing. After the outbreak of the Second World War Upton Fort returned to operational status. Again, only two of the gun positions were made operational, but this time the fit was of two 6 inch guns – ancient weapons from the scrapped battleship HMS *Erin,* which had also seen service with the Turkish Navy as the *Reshadieh* – and these guns were positioned on the former 9.2 inch platforms, with the magazines below once again fulfilling their design purposes. A 4.5 inch howitzer gun of French construction augmented the two naval guns, plus light anti-aircraft weapons. The guns of Upton Fort were the only coastal defence guns on the Dorset foreshore to see action during the war, for on the night of 21st March 1944 they opened fire on marauding enemy E-boats prowling around the edges of Weymouth Bay.

In common with all the UK's coastal gun batteries, Upton Fort was taken out of service in 1956. Today the fort is in private ownership, with the support buildings providing both permanent and holiday homes – all enjoying beautiful coastal views across the bay to the Isle of Portland.

The main (north) entrance to the Verne Citadel, Portland.

A section of the Verne Citadel shortly after its completion in 1881.
Notice the pair of muzzle-loading guns on the ramparts.

VERNE CITADEL

Location: Portland Heights.
OS Reference: SY 691738 (North Gate).
Viewing: Strictly no access to the main citadel (unless visiting a prison inmate!); good distant views against the skyline from many directions and close to from public footpaths around the defensive ditch. Access is permitted to the High Angle Battery.

With Royal Assent having been given a year earlier, work commenced on the building of the Verne Citadel in 1848 on a 48 acre site, nearly 500 feet (152 m) above sea level, on top of the Isle of Portland. As a by-product of the building of the Verne, stone excavated from the defensive ditch (or dry moat) – some 70 feet (21 m) deep and 120 feet (36.6 m) wide at its maximum – was taken back

The entrance to the main magazine at the High Angle Battery. Note the 18 inch gauge rails left from the internal railway track and the date plaque.

down to sea level and used in the construction of the first two arms of the Portland Harbour breakwaters. Ironically, much of the labour for the excavation of the stone came from the nearby Portland Prison – for today the Verne is Portland's prison, and the former purpose-built prison a Young Offenders Institute.

As originally planned, the Verne was to be a heavy artillery base, and was completed as such by 1881. The guns were intended primarily for self-protection in case of seige, but had a secondary role of assisting in the coastal defence of the newly built Portland safe anchorage. However, the muzzle-loading guns (a variety of 12.5 inch, 8 inch and 7 inch weapons) were becoming obsolete even as they were sited and the fort was redesignated as an infantry barracks in 1903, and by 1906 the last of the guns had been moved out.

The main entrance to the citadel is via the impressive archway, complete with portcullis, on its northern side, approached today via Verne Common Road. There is a sallyport on its western side leading to a drawbridge over the ditch, whilst another sallyport to the east provides access to the East Wears Battery some 200 feet (61 m) below.

During the Second World War the Area Coastal Artillery Head-quarters was located within the confines of the Verne and the former magazines used for storage. The Verne's military days were over by the late 1940s and ownership was transferred to the Home Office, which opened the present HM Prison Portland in 1950.

To give better coverage to West Bay it was decided, after successful trials in 1886 converting a standard 9 inch muzzle-loader to fire at a maximum elevation of 70 degrees, to install a battery of guns just to the west of the southern entrance to the citadel. It was known as the High Angle Battery, and was based on the premise that enemy shipping was more vulnerable to plunging shells than those strik-ing horizontally, as upper deck armour was thinner than that on a

Firing drill at one of the turntable mounted howitzers at the
High Angle Battery in about 1900.

vessel's sides. Six turntable mounted, high angle howitzers were installed, capable of firing to the east of Chesil Beach as well as into West Bay, and remote observation posts were established on both sides of Portland (some of which remain to this day).

Also known as the South Flanking Battery, the guns here remained operational until 1907, with the associated shelters and magazines outliving them for many years – as ammunition stores during the Second World War and for artillery weapon storage in the immediate post war years. Today the site is open to the public and is well signposted.

GLOSSARY

BAILEY. The area inside the castle walls, originally the defended yard adjoining the *motte*.

BATTER. The external sloping base of a castle wall, due to the thickening of the masonry (hence 'battering ram').

BARBICAN. A small fortification at a castle entrance, in front of the *gatehouse*.

BASTION. An angled projection from the main castle walls, allowing flanking fire across the faces of the outer walls.

BREECH-LOADER. A gun (normally an artillery piece) in which the shell is loaded at the rear end.

CASEMATE. A vaulted chamber built in to the thickness of the *ramparts*.

CRENELS. The spaces between the *merlons*.

CRENELLATIONS. The battlements pattern capping a castle wall.

CONSTABLE. The person in charge of the castle's defences.

CORBEL. The mounting projecting from a castle wall on which the *machicolations* were positioned.

CURTAIN WALL. Stone wall between the towers.

DITCH. A *moat* without water.

DRAWBRIDGE. A bridge over a *moat* or *ditch* which could be drawn up to prevent access.

EMBRASURE. A bevelled opening in the castle wall providing a sheltered position for the firing of bows or guns.

ENFILADING. Firing along the outer castle walls, rather than away from the castle, most often from a *casemate*.

GARDEROBE. Originally a store-room for valuables, but later generally applied to latrines in the castle.

GATEHOUSE. The fortified gateway to a castle.

GLACIS. A cleared area outside the walls, passing over which an attacking force is vulnerable to defensive fire.

KEEP. A strong tower, usually the safest place in the whole castle and the final point of defence.

LOOPHOLE. A narrow vertical slit in the castle wall (similar to an *embrasure*).

MACHICOLATION. An overhanging gallery from which boiling oil or tar could be poured upon an attacker and from which other, downwards-firing weaponry could be employed.

MERLON. Upright, solid part of the battlements.

MOAT. A wide *ditch,* filled with water, surrounding a castle. **Motte.** A mound of earth on which a tower was built.

MUZZLE-LOADER. A gun into which the shell is loaded at the barrel mouth.

PALISADE. A wooden fence of strong and pointed wooden stakes used to form either a permanent or short- term defensive structure. Often the outer wall of a castle which did not use masonry structures.

PORTCULLIS. A metal grating which could be raised or lowered from within the castle (usually from within the *gatehouse*) to protect an entrance way.

RAMPARTS. A defensive bank of earth, with or without a stone parapet.

RIFLED/RIFLING. Grooves running inside a gun barrel to provide rotation to the shell and, hence, increased accuracy.

WARD. A castle courtyard.

FURTHER READING

Billett, M., *Thatched Buildings of Dorset*, 1984
Broughton, H., *Wareham. Its Interesting History - Ancient and Modern*, 1978
Coker, J., *Survey of Dorset*, 1732
Hardy, F., *The Siege (of Corfe Castle)*, 1984
Hutchins, J., *The History and Antiquities of Dorset* (4 volumes), 1861-1874
HMSO, *Historical Monuments in the County of Dorset* (8 volumes)
Matarasso, F., *The English Castle*, 1995
Morris, S., *Portland, An Illustrated History*, 1985
Page, W., *The Victoria County History of Dorset* (Vol II), 1908
Pomeroy, C., *Military Dorset Today*, 1995
Proceedings of the Dorset Natural History and Archaeological Society
Saunders, A., *Channel Defences*, 1997
The Victoria History of Hampshire and the Isle of Wight (Volumes IV and V),
    1912
Wilton, P., *Castles of Dorset*, 1995
    The specific guide books to the following properties, which are for sale
    at the associated property: Brownsea Island (National Trust), Corfe
    Castle (National Trust), Lulworth Castle (English Heritage), Nothe Fort
    (Weymouth Civic Society), Portland Castle (English Heritage), Sherborne
    Old Castle (English Heritage).

ACKNOWLEDGEMENTS

Most of the photographs for this book were taken by the author, but Colin Pomeroy would like to thank the following for allowing the inclusion of illustrations in their possession or for which they hold the copyright. Cambridge University Collection of Air Photographs: pages 26, 30, 33. Dorset County Museum: page 11. Dovecote Press: copyright page, pages 16, 17, 34, 40, 44, 45, 52, 53, 56 (top). Stuart Morris: pages 64, 71, 73. Royal Commission Historical Monuments (England), © Crown Copyright: frontispiece, pages 8, 18, 19, 35, 39, 51.

The

DISCOVER DORSET

Series of Books

A series of paperback books providing informative illustrated
introductions to Dorset's history, culture and way of life.
The following titles have so far been published.

All the books about Dorset published by The Dovecote Press
are available in bookshops throughout the county,
or in case of difficulty direct from the publishers.
The Dovecote Press Ltd, Stanbridge,
Wimborne, Dorset BH21 4JD
Tel: 01258 840549 www.dovecotepress.com